# Maths skills

### Shirley Clarke & Barry Silsby

### Illustrated by Sascha Lipscomb

BROCKHAMPTON PRESS
LONDON

## NOTES FOR PARENTS

Research has shown that when children and parents work together at home, the child's work at school improves.

The purpose of the *Headstart* books is to provide activities which your child will enjoy doing and which will encourage learning to take place in the home.

You can help your child get the most out of this book by:

- *talking about the activities,* without 'telling' your child how to do them. Encourage your child to think of different ways of working things out.
- *reading the advice below.* This gives further information and explains the purpose of each activity.
- *letting your child control the pace* of working through the book. Too many pages in one go may put your child off.
- *giving lots of praise and encouragement.* Children get better at subjects they believe they are good at.

**Pages 4 – 5  Shape experiment**
By physically handling 3D shapes, your child can take time to count faces and edges ('sides' apply to 2D shapes only). By rolling and stacking the shapes your child is finding out more about them, which will lead to an appreciation of why certain shapes are used in different environments such as industry.

**Pages 6 – 7  Do you agree?**
This activity is meant to be a fun means of collecting and interpreting data. Some of the statements (like 'hunting is cruel') could lead to interesting discussions amongst the members of your family. Other statements (like 'the tooth fairy does not leave enough money') will prompt fairly predictable responses, depending on whether a child or an adult is being asked the question. It is important that your child feels in control of the data he or she has gathered. Encourage him or her to draw conclusions from it (for example, maybe more help could be given around the house).

**Pages 8 – 9  Symmetry grids**
This activity introduces patterns with two lines of symmetry, where your child has an active role in 'creating' symmetrical patterns. Encourage your child to colour the grids in faintly at first, in case of mistakes, so that they can be rubbed out easily.

 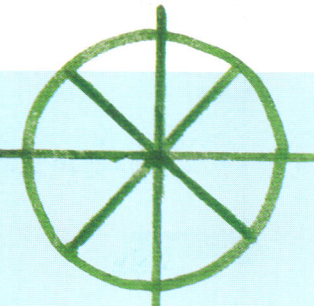 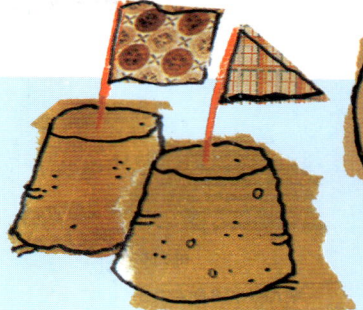 

### Pages 10 – 11   Treasure hunt
This game aims to help your child learn the directions of the compass points: north, south, east and west. The grid can be used again and again, with different treasure hunts.

### Pages 12 – 13   Will it, won't it?
This fun activity will help your child with the notion of probability, and will cause a few laughs!

### Pages 14 – 15   Sort it out
Children are often asked to sort shapes, but this activity asks them to decide how someone else has sorted the shapes on the page. You may need to talk through the activity with your child, until he or she grasps the idea of identifying properties. Ask questions like, 'What is the same about all of these shapes?' and, 'In what way are all of these shapes different from all of these?'

### Pages 16 – 17   Headstart quiz
These questions aim to do more than just test general maths knowledge. Some of the answers will provide new information for your child.

### Pages 18 – 19   Don't be a litterbug!
This game aims to teach children the directions of the compass points. It also has the potential for encouraging some strategic thinking, as the choice of starting place is important if you do not want to miss too many goes. As two of the compass points have been left out (because a dice has only six faces), you could swap them in to vary the games you play.

### Pages 20 – 21   Decisions, decisions
This activity will encourage your child to make decisions about probability. The need for some objects will depend on your circumstances (for example, if you always go to the swimming pool in the car, you probably won't need the bike). In any cases of this kind, the statement will have to go in the middle column.

### Pages 22 – 23   Going shopping
This activity involves two things: completing a graph from the given information in the book, and then constructing a graph after collecting some information. Your child can collect this information in two ways: either by asking, 'What is your favourite fruit?' or by asking, 'What is your favourite fruit out of these - apple, orange, banana or pear ?' (or a similar limited list). Either way will produce interesting results.

### Pages 24 – 25   Symmetry search
Symmetry exists all around us, not just in maths. The Alhambra Palace tile patterns are famous for their geometric beauty. This activity aims to help your child identify several lines of symmetry, and also appreciate the beauty of geometric mathematics. Use a small mirror to help you check that your child has put the lines in the right place.

### Pages 26 – 27   Time off
This spread involves interpreting data from a timetable.

### Pages 28 – 29   Family favourites
The object of data handling and surveys is to be able to interpret the results for a particular purpose. The purpose of this survey is to look for similarities and differences in the preferences of males and females. If there are no patterns in the data your child obtains (because every one in the family gives a different response), suggest that he or she asks the family to choose their favourite meal, colour etc. from a list of four.

### Pages 30 – 31   Database
Accessing information from a database involves finding out new things from a set of statistics. The data in this spread tells us which clubs are most popular for boys and girls, and whether the day of the week affects attendance at the clubs.

 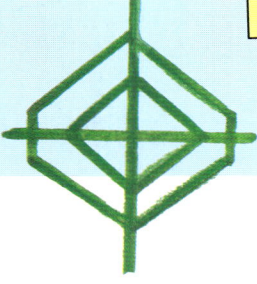   

# Shape experiment

Find some of these shapes in your home.

**cubes**
(such as square boxes or stock cubes)

**cuboids**
(such as long boxes or cereal packets)

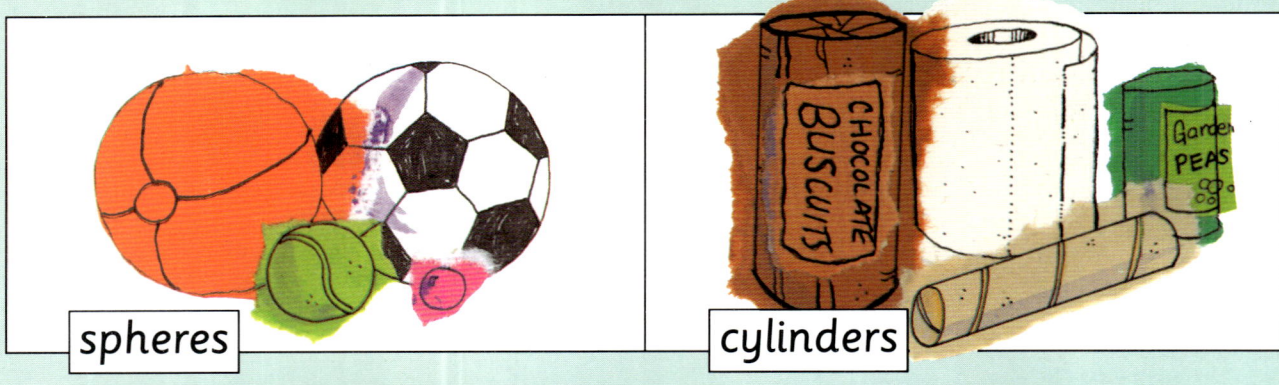

**spheres**
(such as tennis balls or footballs)

**cylinders**
(such as kitchen rolls or toilet roll centres)

Now try these experiments with your shapes.

1   Find out which shapes **roll**. Tick (✔) those that **do**.

2   Find out which shapes **stack**. Tick (✔) those that **do**.

3   Find out which shapes have **six faces**. Tick (✔) those that **do**.

4   Find out which shapes have **two edges or less**. Tick (✔) those that **do**.

Now find out something about the shapes for yourself.

I have ticked those shapes which

# Do you agree?

How well do you, your family and your friends agree with one another? Here's a survey to find out!

**1** First decide whether *you* agree or disagree with each of the statements on the opposite page. Fill in one of the columns of the chart with your answers.

**2** Now ask some of your family and friends whether they agree or disagree with the statements. Fill in their answers on the chart. Put a ✔ if they agree and a ✘ if they disagree.

**3** Count how many people agreed and how many people disagreed with each statement. Write the number in the total column.

Now answer these questions:

- Are there any statements you all agree with? _____

- Are there any statements you all disagree with? _____

- Are there any statements that all the adults agree with and all the children disagree with? _____

- Are there any statements that all the children agree with and all the adults disagree with? _____

|  | Name | | Name | | Name | | Name | | Name | | Name | | Name | | TOTAL | |
|---|---|---|---|---|---|---|---|---|---|---|---|---|---|---|---|---|
|  | ✓ | ✗ | ✓ | ✗ | ✓ | ✗ | ✓ | ✗ | ✓ | ✗ | ✓ | ✗ | ✓ | ✗ | ✓ | ✗ |
| Hunting is cruel. | | | | | | | | | | | | | | | | |
| It is better to feel too hot than too cold. | | | | | | | | | | | | | | | | |
| Television is good for you. | | | | | | | | | | | | | | | | |
| Cabbage is disgusting. | | | | | | | | | | | | | | | | |
| Pets are a nuisance. | | | | | | | | | | | | | | | | |
| To get rid of hiccups, hold your breath. | | | | | | | | | | | | | | | | |
| Counting goes on forever. | | | | | | | | | | | | | | | | |
| Holidays are fun. | | | | | | | | | | | | | | | | |
| The tooth fairy doesn't leave enough money. | | | | | | | | | | | | | | | | |
| Children should help around the home. | | | | | | | | | | | | | | | | |

7

# Symmetry grids

Colour in the other half of this grid to make a symmetrical pattern. Use exactly the same colours as in the book.

The line down the middle of the grid is called a **line of symmetry.**

Now colour in this grid where the line of symmetry is in a different place.

This pattern has two lines of symmetry.

Look carefully at how the pattern is symmetrical in two ways.

Now colour in these patterns with two lines of symmetry.

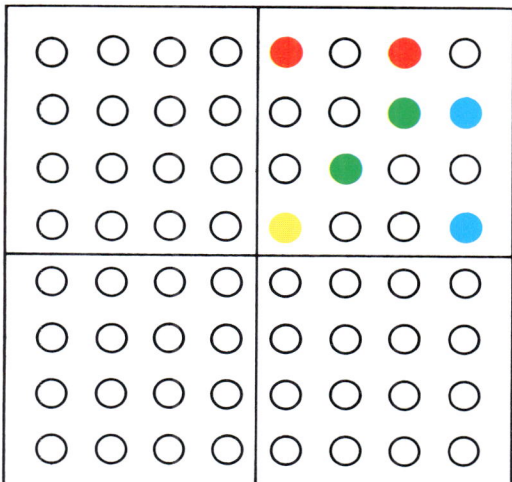

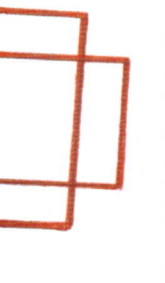

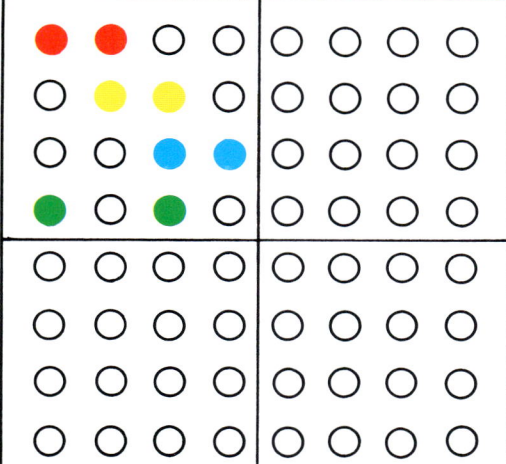

You might find it easier if you turn the book around as you go!

Use this grid to make a symmetrical pattern of your own. Draw in your pattern's lines of symmetry.

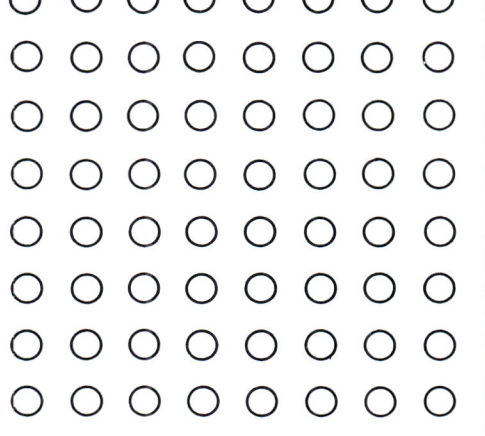

# Treasure hunt

Follow the route to find the treasure!

Put a counter on start and follow the instructions.
(The compass will help you.)

Find out which square the treasure is hidden in.

1. Go N 3 squares.
2. Go E 4 squares.
3. Go N 1 square.
4. Go W 2 squares.
5. Go S 4 squares.
6. Go E 2 squares.
7. Go N 6 squares.
8. Go W 3 squares.

The treasure is in square number ☐

Now try this different treasure hunt:

1. Go E 4 squares.
2. Go N 1 square.
3. Go W 2 squares.
4. Go N 3 squares.
5. Go W 1 square.
6. Go E 3 squares.
7. Go N 2 squares.
8. Go S 4 squares.

The treasure is in square number ☐

Answers on page 32.

Why not make up your own treasure hunt and ask your family or friends to solve it?

# Will it, won't it?

Decide whether each of these statements:

- is impossible
- might happen
- is certain

Draw a line from each statement to the right box.

Someone in the world will be born on the same day as me.

A six month old baby will win the high jump competition in the Olympics.

My mum will meet the Queen of England.

is impossible

Rabbits will all lose their tails tomorrow.

I shall be famous one day.

# Sort it out

These robots sort shapes in different ways. They have created a shape challenge for you.

Look carefully at the shapes below and see if you can find out how they sorted these shapes.

Turn the book upside-down to see if you got it right.

They are sorted into shapes which have 3 sides and shapes which do not have 3 sides. (Or: shapes which are triangles and shapes which are not triangles.)

Now try these robot shape challenges!

1 | do have | do not have |

2 | do have | do not have |

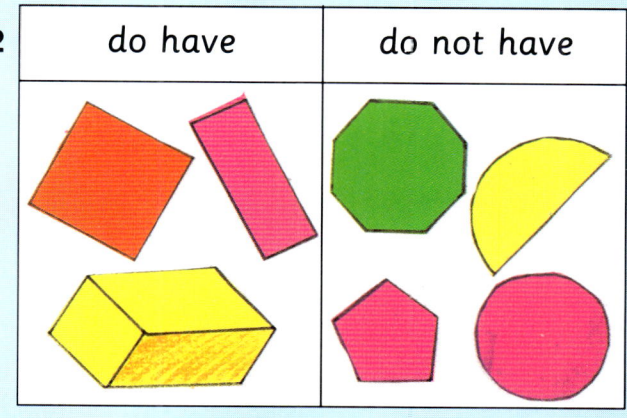

Make one up of your own here:

3 | do have | do not have |

4 | do have | do not have |

Answers on page 32.

15

# Headstart quiz

How many of the questions can you answer?

**HEADStart**
Is this an octagon?
1

**HEADStart**
Which direction is opposite NW?
2

**HEADStart**
What is the name of a shape with six sides?
3

**HEADStart**
How many faces have three cubes?
4

**HEADStart**
Which of these animals is grey and heavy with small ears?
1 An elephant.
2 A rhinoceros.
3 A mouse.
5

# Don't be a litterbug!

Here's a game for two or more people to play.
The playground is full of rubbish which needs picking up.

## You need

10 small pieces of scrunched-up paper (smaller than the squares opposite).
A counter for each player.    A die.

    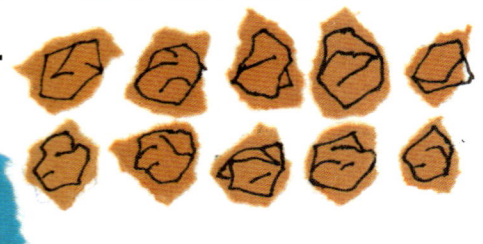

How to play:
- Place the scraps of paper on ten squares of your choice.
- Choose where you want to put your counter to start.
- Throwing the die, move your counter as shown opposite.
- Pick up any paper in any square you land on.
- The first player to pick up five pieces of paper is the winner.
- If you can't move, miss a go.

This compass will help you.

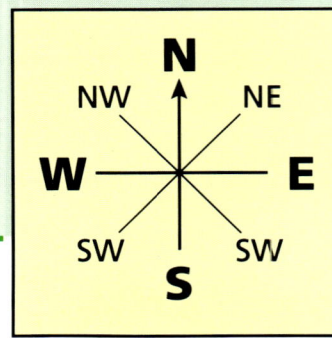

## How to move

- Go N one square
- Go S one square
- Go SE one square
- Go E one square
- Go W one square
- Go NW one square

Play this game several times. Where is the best place to start so you don't have to miss too many goes?

# Decisions, decisions

Imagine you are going swimming. Which of the things in the picture opposite would you:

- definitely need;
- possibly need;
- definitely not need?

Write the name of each item in the correct column below.

| definitely need | possibly need | definitely not need |
|---|---|---|
|  |  |  |

Has anything been left out of the lists?
If you can think of anything else, write it in.

# Going shopping

8 apples
15 satsumas
10 pears
8 bananas
2 oranges

Look at the lady's shopping list.

Which is the most popular fruit in her family?

_____

How many fruits altogether is
she going to have to carry home?  ☐ fruits

Which fruits are equally popular with the family?

_____

Draw a graph to show the popularity of fruit in the lady's family.

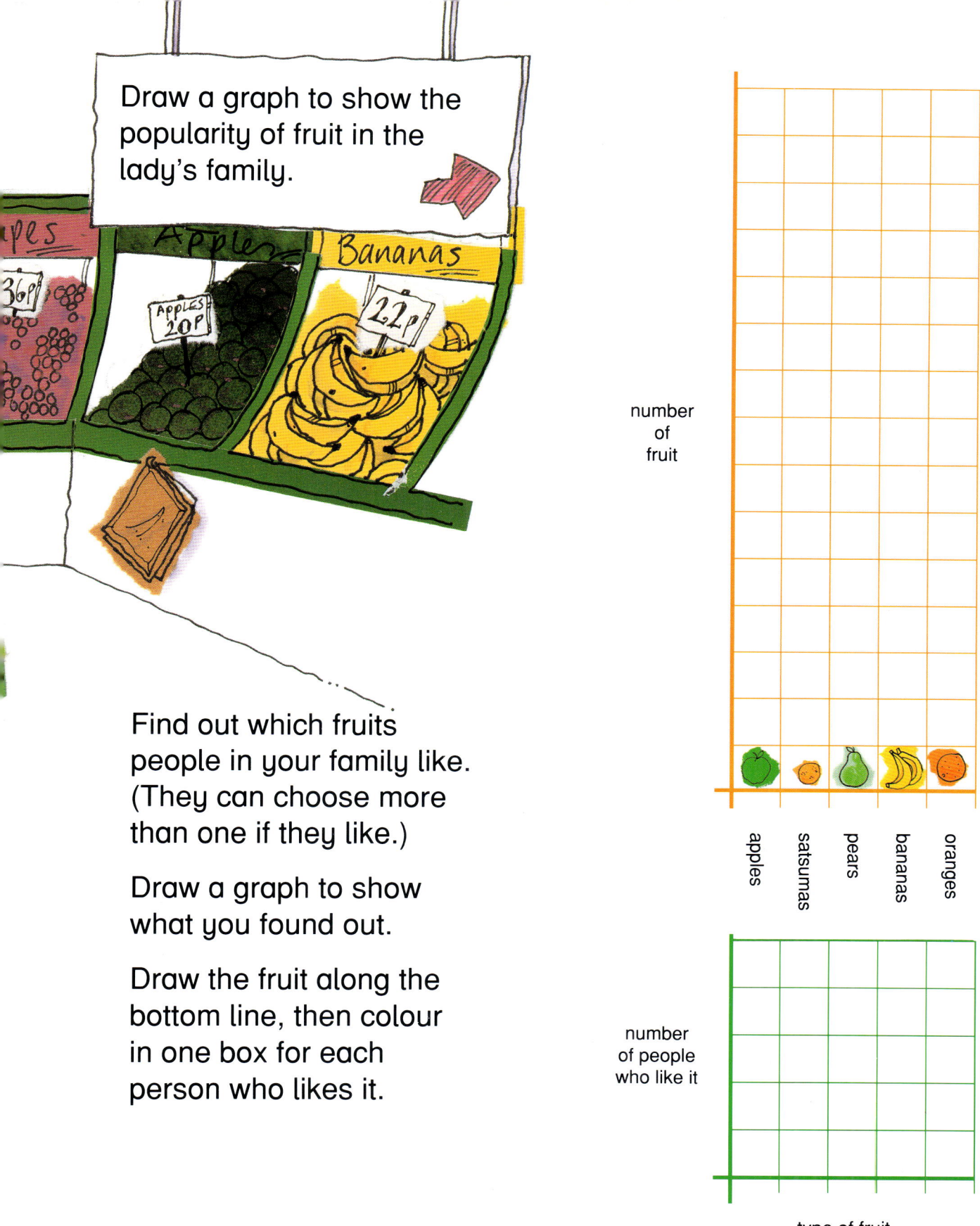

Find out which fruits people in your family like. (They can choose more than one if they like.)

Draw a graph to show what you found out.

Draw the fruit along the bottom line, then colour in one box for each person who likes it.

Which fruit is the most popular in your family?

# Symmetry search

These patterns come from the tiles in the Alhambra Palace in Spain. They all have one or more lines of symmetry.

This pattern has one line of symmetry, because the middle strip is woven through the middle hexagon.

This pattern has two lines of symmetry.

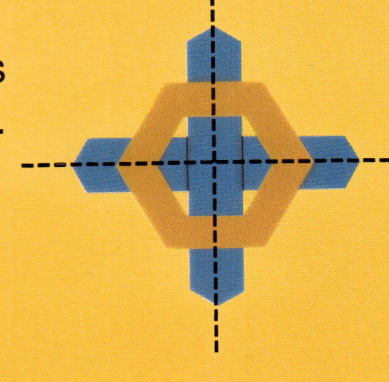

### Remember

A line of symmetry has a perfect reflection on either side of it. You can check by putting the edge of a small mirror on the lines of symmetry that are drawn in. Is the reflection the same as the pattern in the book?

Can you draw one or more lines of symmetry on each of the patterns opposite?
Use a small mirror to help you.  Answers on page 32.

# Time off

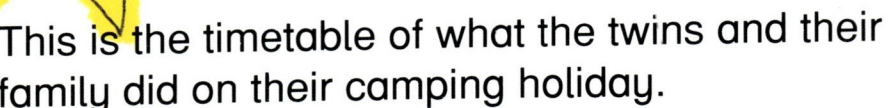

This is the timetable of what the twins and their family did on their camping holiday.

| Monday | | | |
|---|---|---|---|
| a.m. Arrive at Campsite | p.m. Boat trip round the harbour |
| **Tuesday** | | | |
| a.m. All day on the beach | p.m. |
| **Wednesday** | | | |
| a.m. Visit smuggling museum | p.m. Amusement park |

| Thursday | | | |
|---|---|---|---|
| a.m. Swimming | p.m. Visit the lighthouse |
| **Friday** | | | |
| a.m. All day walk to the castle and back | p.m. |
| **Saturday** | | | |
| a.m. Shopping for souvenirs | p.m. Pack up and leave |

Look at the timetable and answer these questions:

- How many days were the family on holiday? _____

- When did they go to the museum? _____

- On which days did they need a packed lunch? _____

- Write down two more facts about the twins' holiday.

  1 _____

  2 _____

Supposing you could go anywhere and do anything you liked on holiday. Fill in your ideal holiday timetable.

| Day | a.m. | p.m. |
|---|---|---|
| Monday | | |
| Tuesday | | |
| Wednesday | | |
| Thursday | | |
| Friday | | |
| Saturday | | |

# Family favourites

Carry out a survey of your family to find out each person's favourite colour, meal, sport, hobby and pop star.

| name | favourite colour | favourite meal | favourite sport | favourite hobby |
|---|---|---|---|---|
|  |  |  |  |  |
|  |  |  |  |  |
|  |  |  |  |  |
|  |  |  |  |  |
|  |  |  |  |  |
|  |  |  |  |  |

| favourite pop star |
|---|
| ............. |
| ............. |
| ............. |
| ............. |
| ............. |

Did you get the same answer from everyone for any question?

_____

If yes, which one? _____

Can you see any patterns for males and females (such as all the males liking the same colour or all the females liking the same sport)?

_____

_____

What else have you discovered from your survey?

_____

_____

# Database

This computer shows how many boys and girls attend different clubs in their town.

| HOBBY | BOYS | GIRLS | EVENING |
|---|---|---|---|
| youth club | 152 | 135 | Fri |
| judo | 72 | 130 | Wed |
| drama | 40 | 35 | Mon |
| dancing | 10 | 52 | Mon |
| chess | 15 | 19 | Fri |
| swimming | 27 | 72 | Thur |

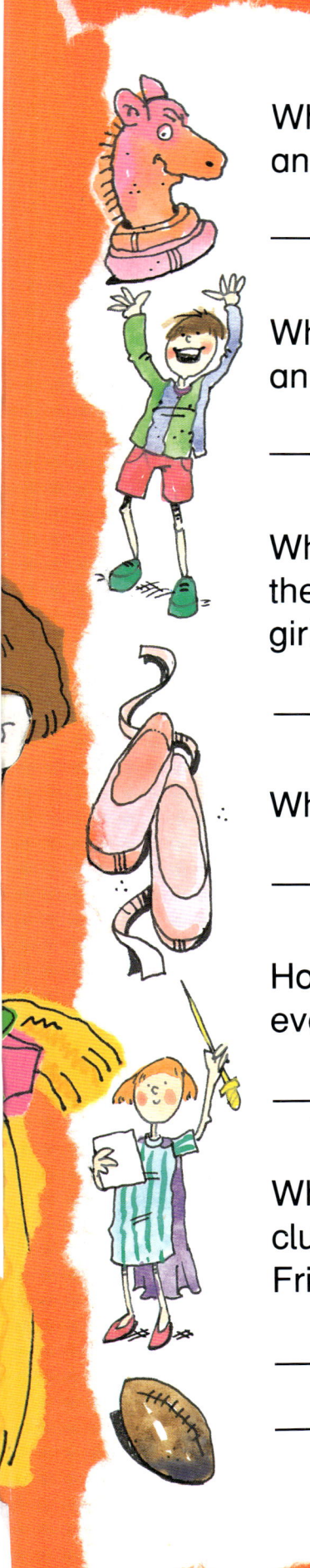

Which clubs need to attract more boys to make an even number of boys and girls?

_____

Which clubs need to attract more girls to make an even number of boys and girls?

_____

Which club has the biggest difference between the number of boy members and the number of girl members?

_____

Which club is the most popular in the town?

_____

How many children attend clubs on a Monday evening?

_____

Why might only a few children attend the chess club on a Friday? (Clue: what else happens on Friday?)

_____

_____

# ANSWERS

### Pages 4–5 Shape experiment
1 The cylinder and sphere roll.
2 The cube, cuboid and cylinder stack.
3 The cube and cuboid have 6 faces.
4 The cylinder and sphere have 2 edges or less.

### Pages 10–11 Treasure hunt
The treasure is in square numbers 2 and 29.

### Pages 14–15 Sort it out
1 All the shapes have curves.
2 All the shapes have square corners.
3 All the shapes are symmetrical or regular.

### Pages 16–17 Headstart quiz
1 Yes, octagons must have 8 sides.
2 SE (south-east).
3 A hexagon.
4 18.
5 A rhinoceros.
6 27.
7 No, it looks symmetrical, but no human being has identical sides of the body.
8 A cuboid.
9 7.
10 A pentagon.

### Pages 24–25
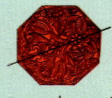  
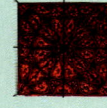  

---

British Library Cataloguing in Publication Data
Clarke, Shirley
 Headstart: Maths Skills: 7–9 — (Headstart)
 I. Title  II. Silsby, Barry
 372.7

ISBN 1-86019-526-1

This edition published 1997 by Brockhampton Press, a member of Hodder Headline PLC Group.
10 9 8 7 6 5 4 3
1999 1998 1997

© 1991 Shirley Clarke and Barry Silsby

All rights reserved. No part of this publication may be reproduced or transmitted in any form or by any means, electronic or mechanical, including photocopy, recording, or any information storage and retrieval system, without permission in writing from the publisher or under licence from the Copyright Licensing Agency Limited. Further details of such licences (for reprographic reproduction) may be obtained from the Copyright Licensing Agency Limited, of 90 Tottenham Court Road, London W1P 9HE.

Typeset by Oxprint, Oxford OX2 6TR.
Printed in India.